F. Novotny

CÉZANNE

PHAIDON

Phaidon Press Limited, Littlegate House, St Ebbe's Street, Oxford
Published in the United States of America by E. P. Dutton, New York

First published 1961
Third edition 1972
Reprinted with corrections 1978
Reprinted 1979

© 1976 Elsevier Publishing Projects, Lausanne

ISBN 0 7148 1535 7
Library of Congress Catalog Card Number: 70-157133

Printed in Great Britain by Morrison & Gibb Ltd, Edinburgh

CÉZANNE

Now that we have reached the second half of the twentieth century, it ought to be possible, when we look back upon the development of art during the nineteenth century, to establish some semblance of order amidst the manifold and confusing ramifications of artistic activity during that epoch. The 'historical distance' is great enough to enable us to perceive with clarity the relationship between the various phases of development, but it is not yet great enough for the remoteness of time to have added to the essential characteristics of works of art that quality which colours our views of all the productions of older art. We feel that all the most important artistic events of the nineteenth century are easily accessible to our understanding. We feel that we can experience, as if it were a work of the present day, every picture painted during that period, tracing it back to the primary motives which inspired it.

From our present-day point of view we are bound to consider the unparalleled many-sidedness of art as an enduring characteristic of the previous century. In the development of older art it is impossible to find a similar contrast to that offered us by the end of the nineteenth century, when Van Gogh painted the 'portrait' of a chair while another leading artist, Cézanne, was eliminating even from the representation of the human countenance every trace of psychology and feeling. Nor is it likely that remoter posterity will take a different view.

At the same time we recognize a unifying fundamental characteristic: the tendency towards representation of the elemental. This tendency, in the form of demonstration of elementary forces or elementary images, was one of the chief aims nineteenth-century painting strove to achieve. It appears with ever-increasing prominence as the fundamental theme to which all other formative intentions were subordinated.

No other artist had such an important share in this movement as Paul Cézanne. With the formula of artistic representation of the elemental, however inadequate and universal it may be in itself, it is possible to establish the comprehensive and fundamental character of this complicated artistic personality, and starting from this basis we are able to understand the numerous problems of representation which the paintings of Cézanne bring before us.

Elementary images can be created only by sacrificing the individual phenomena, the individual value of the human figure, the tree, the still-life subject, etc. Anyone who sees pictures by Cézanne for the first time, and is impressed by the effect they produce, will be struck when he thinks of the forms of nature depicted, by certain characteristic and surprising phenomena of reduction, which awaken his critical consciousness. An exception must perhaps be made in the case of those who are particularly susceptible to colour, for they will recognize at once that the colour quality of these works is something unique. They will find in Cézanne a power and exclusiveness of chromatic effect for which few parallels can be found among the works of older art; we could go even farther; they will find colours and combinations of colours possessing characteristics which differentiate Cézanne's chromatics from all other kinds of colour-treatment. Actually, those who can see this have grasped the essential point of Cézanne's artistic genius, from which all his processes of representation and form-conception are derived. To such observers it will appear natural to allow this incomparable harmony of colours to produce its effects alone; its laws will be felt or recognized, and everything else which is to be seen in the picture seems, by comparison, to possess only secondary importance. The perfection of colouring, of colour organisms, which they recognize Cézanne's works to be, appears to them as an adequate justification of all other peculiarities of representation, and they are tempted to think that more exhaustive investigation of these peculiarities is futile.

To assume such an attitude towards Cézanne's art would, however, be quite wrong, however much we may be tempted to do so by many of its forms of expression. To regard a picture by Cézanne merely as an ornament in colour would mean that we were overlooking certain essential effective elements, and, more especially, certain very significant creative processes in his art. In reality this art is so constituted that the beholder must constantly take into consideration its realistic, illustrative value, just as the artist, when he was painting his pictures, had constantly before his eyes the objects of nature he was depicting. If we do this, we are at once struck by those phenomena of reduction which are very characteristic peculiarities of all Cézanne's work and distinguish it most profoundly from the immediately preceding art of the Impressionists. In its essentials the art of Cézanne is close to nature and tends towards reality. Even many of his watercolours and certain oil paintings from his late period with their forms of intimation and abstraction cannot be taken as evidence of 'abstract' painting. Nevertheless there is one characteristic of Cézanne's mode of representation which one may describe superficially as aloofness from life, or, more profoundly and comprehensively, as aloofness from mankind; it is this characteristic which gives his pictures, for those who approach them for the first time, a cold, rigid, almost repugnant character, and renders their comprehension difficult for many people. This aloofness is naturally most evident in Cézanne's representation of the human figure, which, as a matter of fact, plays just as important a part in the totality of his art as other natural objects, landscape or still-life. In Cézanne's pictures the human figure often has an almost puppet-like rigidity, while the countenances show an emptiness of expression bordering almost on the mask. Corresponding characteristics are to be found in his representation of all other kinds of subjects. As if all his landscapes – in which human figures hardly ever appear – were depicted in a complete absence of wind, his foliage and sheets of water are quite motionless. The expressiveness of motionless organic life, too, as we perceive it for instance in the rhythm of branches and leaves, is generally subdued in Cézanne and produces no direct effect, while when we turn to the objects of inorganic nature we find that these too are characterized by a rigidity which goes beyond their natural immobility. This reduction of movement and natural animation is not confined to the corporeal world but is extended to atmospheric phenomena and lighting. Certainly aerial perspective exists in Cézanne's pictures, but the depth values of the various remote portions of the pictorial space do not give the effect of being everywhere in harmony with the atmospheric haziness. One has rather the impression that the contemplation of the atmospheric effects has not been definitely considered as a problem of painting. This is due chiefly to the peculiar nature of the colours, of which we cannot say whether they are atmospheric colours, as in impressionistic painting, or local colours. In this way, with the lack of atmospheric effects in Cézanne's pictures, especially in his landscapes, a further source of animation is missing. A similar peculiarity may be noticed in his representation of light. As with the atmosphere, he does not seem to have made the representation of light in easily recognizable forms and situations of illumination a subject for special study. The result of this in Cézanne's pictures is often the appearance of a neutral, somewhat timeless lighting, and this has led to the supposition that, when possible, he tried to paint his landscapes in a diffuse light, under an overcast sky. In reality, however, most of his landscapes, especially those he painted in Provence, are in sunlight, but the sunlight is hardly ever reproduced in such a way as to be distributed evenly over the whole landscape. In particular it is the cast shadows which, like all the colours and line images throughout Cézanne's work, in the neighbourhood of clearly marked patches often display an indistinctness and a tendency to fade away which is difficult to explain, so that the impression of continuous lighting cannot predominate.

An elementary phenomenon of space too, such as linear perspective, is subjected in Cézanne's pictures to processes of transformation which contribute to the reduction of natural animation. It is true that on the whole he follows the laws of perspective, conceiving the pictorial plane as perspectival space, but he reduces to a minimum the effects of tension, which in real landscape are always bound up with perspectival contrasts of dimension, with foreshortenings and converging lines. In Cézanne's representation of space we have the unique phenomenon of a perspective so to speak emptied of feeling, the peculiarities of which consist of occasional changes of angle, displacement of proportions and axes, and especially of a curious hesitation in the movement of the converging lines and absence of tension in the perspectival depth.

Lastly there is one more characteristic of Cézanne's art which may be mentioned at the end of this résumé. In his representation there is a lack of pleasure in the reproduction of substance, or at least in the direct reproduction of material beauties. The illuminating power of the colours of flower and fruit in Cézanne's still-lifes is only to a slight degree effective as material beauty; similarly the clear landscape distance in many of his pictures cannot be felt as the clarity of determined meteorological conditions. In consequence his objects have a kind of immateriality; despite the solidity of their corporeal and spatial structure, they seem to be without weight, when compared, for example, with the sensuality of impressionistic renderings.

At the bottom of all these characteristics, which embrace a wide range from psychological content in the representation of the human figure to the elemental forms of space, is what we have described above as aloofness from mankind and from life. To this fundamental attitude belongs also the lack of everything that we understand by the German word 'Stimmung' in its widest sense, a term for which there is no equivalent in English, but which can best be rendered by the English word 'mood' or 'atmosphere'. The element of mood, which is found in some form or other in all European landscape paintings from the beginnings until the end of impressionism and which before the appearance of Cézanne seems to be an indispensable part of the interpretation of landscape, is completely excluded from his landscapes. In them there is no mood, whether in the form of expression of temperament or for the purpose of interpreting definite landscape situations or phenomena, and it is lacking because Cézanne's art is the very antithesis of expressive art.

So much of these fundamental characteristics has passed into the artistic tendencies of our own century that we are already familiar with them. Their first appearance, however – and in many ways their purest form – in the art of Cézanne marks a turning-point of the highest importance in the history of intellectual development.

Strangely enough, those peculiar elements of Cézanne's paintings are frequently disputed; indeed, an observer who might happen to remark on the peculiar, unlifelike stiffness of most of Cézanne's portraits is met by an assiduous insistence upon the great expressiveness of Cézanne's mode of representation. But to recognize all the ways in which natural phenomena of external and internal life are here disregarded is certainly not the same as to belittle Cézanne's art. This art, too, is an example of the fact that those who criticize it are often better aware of quite obvious phenomena than those who defend it. Not everyone who is surprised at the coldness of expression in Cézanne's pictures, at the lack of attractive elements, at the slanting houses, the 'angular' ellipses of the fruit dishes and the deformed nudes, has less understanding of this style of painting than one who is no longer surprised. It would, of course, be a mistake to think that Cézanne's artistic experience was altogether devoid of emotional content such as the expression animating a face, the mood inspired by a landscape, the material beauty and secret life of a *nature morte*. In a portrait such as that of the *Old Woman with a Rosary* (now in the National Gallery, London) with its heavy, sombre colours, one can really see a picture of old age and decay, of life approaching its end; a landscape such as the '*Jas de Bouffan' in Springtime* is a spring landscape; the most cursory survey of Cézanne's work proves that the Montagne Sainte-Victoire was more to him than a motif for his brush and how much he was attached to the landscape of his native Provence. Even clearer is the thematic importance of many of his figure compositions, in which the 'romantic' side of his nature asserts itself again and again. But all these traits, these manifestations of a thematic and psychological importance, play a very peculiar part in the final result of his creative activity: they are overlaid, overborne by those effects tending in the opposite direction which are certainly much too complicated to be adequately described by terms such as aloofness from life or from mankind. Even a brief comparison with the mode of representation practised by the Impressionists before and during his career shows how much they absorbed the moods and emotional values of landscape phenomena and also of the human model, and how different were the aims of representation in Cézanne's art.

One of the leading characteristics of Cézanne's art is the new kind of relationship between the illusion value of the representation and the impression which the picture creates as a structural form. If we compare it with examples of impressionism, a picture by Cézanne is to a much higher degree a structural form. This is due only to a small extent to the fact that objects are reproduced in a simplified form, with frequent omission of individual details. Much more important than such transformations of objects – which, *nota bene*, are found in varying degrees – is the relationship between pictorial plane and space. Strictly speaking, apart from a few isolated exceptions, no analogy to Cézanne's treatment of space can be found in earlier painting. The phenomena of reduction and attenuation in the perspective effects, in the reproduction of atmosphere and light, are derived from the comprehensive characteristic that space in Cézanne's pictures is not illusory space in the ordinary sense. The pictorial plane contributes too much as an artistic reality to the impression produced by this treatment of space. This, however, does not mean that Cézanne's pictures can be called 'flat'. They are not flat in the sense that they have only a limited extension in depth, nor do they give the flat impression of decorative painting. On the contrary, space does exist in his pictures, but a form of space which despite its depth and intensity nevertheless makes it difficult for the beholder to enter into the spatial construction. The various kinds of sentiment-reduction, in the representation of human figures and objects, of superficial beauty and spatial perspective, find their counterpart in this characteristic of pictorial space: Cézanne aims at reproducing real space – and not super-real space as created in the fantasy of the artist – and nevertheless endeavours to remain aloof from and inaccessible to that contemplative and re-experiencing imagination which tries to follow up the movements of space and extensions of depth in the picture and to identify itself with the perspectival sensations of the bend in a road or the view of a valley.

Cézanne's pictorial structure, which produces this curious effect of space, is thus fundamentally different from other kinds of visible pictorial form – to take an obvious example, from the impressionistic painting method. The form of projection, emphasizing just as much and often even more strongly the plane of the picture, of impressionistic brushwork stands likewise in a relationship of tension to the depth of space depicted, but it is an attractive tension which helps to increase the illusion and to give animation and movement to the spatial picture. Impressionistic painteresque forms of indication and reduction aim at causing the plane of the picture to be forgotten, but in Cézanne's construction the plane is effective even in a fully rounded-off oil painting. Among the means which Cézanne employs to attain his novel construction, two are of especial importance: colour and draughtsmanship.

A philosophy of colour, the aim of which was to demonstrate the elementary laws of colour-effects and above all the essential power of colour, could find no more suitable subject for study than Cézanne's treatment of colour. One cannot investigate it without soon coming upon original phenomena of which it is possible to define the effects, but not the causes. Among the fundamental characteristics of Cézanne's colouring its faculty of creating forms and space must be emphasized. The exclusiveness of this faculty is greater than in all earlier painting, and he relies less than any of his predecessors on other means of representation and form, such as composition and outline-drawing, in obtaining the realization of his conception of the object and solidity of the picture. The latter, especially, is obtained by the equivalence and balance of the individual component colours. These individual patches of colour, as small constructional parts of the picture, are the real supports of the pictorial structure in Cézanne's painting. And it should be noticed that this is found for the first time in Cézanne, for the impressionistic technique of streaks and patches was employed in the service of an individualized reproduction, rich in details, of objects and space, and secondly this painteresque molecular structure, which reduced the value of the individual object, had yet a material significance: the atmosphere inundated with light. The structure on the basis of small component parts, as evolved in the painting of Cézanne, first marks the completion of this movement, which in the course of the development of European painting led farther and farther away from that pictorial world composed of independent objects and individual forms. The predominance of formal and especially of chromatic combinations over the individual bodies depicted, whether living beings or inanimate images, now becomes much stronger, because there was no longer any concrete counterpart, such as the atmosphere, to this painteresque conception of the elemental. This gives rise to the often noticed impression that in Cézanne's pictures the objects appear to form themselves before our eyes, to grow out of the surface of the picture and to dissolve themselves in it again. From this form of painting are derived many curious and important consequences for all the means of form and representation, which had previously been used for the construction of individual bodies, for the drawing of outlines, for modelling and composition. In all of them, when we compare them with other methods of representation, even with the methods of 'painteresque' painting, processes of transformation of values can be recognized which are equivalent to reductions of values.

Let us first consider the outlines. Cézanne's remarks concerning his contempt for line have been quoted so often, in support of the assertion that draughtsmanship was of secondary importance in his work, and, even more, to emphasize the statement that he was incapable of drawing, that it is as well to draw attention to certain examples which contradict these assertions. It is not difficult to find examples of Cézanne's absorption in drawing and of his ability as a draughtsman, particularly in the sketches he made from works of sculpture. Where, however, in Cézanne's drawing, things appear which are the opposite of linear rhythm, of accurate draughtsmanship and animation of line, in the often coarse and clumsy outlines of many of his nudes, in the simplified contours with their varying firmness such as are characteristic of Cézanne's representation as a whole – in all these cases we must recognize that we have to do with a form of outline which is suited to the general structure of the picture. Everywhere in the whole plane of the picture neighbouring units and modulations of colour are found balancing and contrasting with one another, and this finds its counterpart in a form of outline the aim of which is not so much to isolate the object it encloses as to form the connecting link between two contiguous colour-values. Hence the hesitation, hence the continual reappearance and dying away of outlines in Cézanne's painting, the blurring of the contours which do not everywhere correspond to real reflected or cast shadows. The use of outline as a line of demarcation between colours in this painting was bound to present numerous difficulties and obstacles. In the watercolours, in which the soft colour-patches toning down the graphic element in the drawing are often the most important or even the only portions of colour, the construction is concentrated precisely on these most difficult portions. Even the black-and-white form of pure pencil-drawings contains much of this peculiar treatment of outline, so that the relationship between plane and space even in drawings of this kind is similar to that found in the paintings.

With this kind of outline-drawing the possibility of a painteresque modelling is excluded *a priori*. The replacement of modelling by 'modulation' of colours, which the master demanded in a celebrated saying, is very closely connected with Cézanne's system of outlines. The intensification of the colours in the neighbourhood of the contours, however great the resulting plastic effect, is entirely different, as a form of pictorial structure, from modelling.

Cézanne's 'molecular', painteresque pictorial structure, which denies the independent value of individual images, had a particularly strong influence on his composition. The composition, that is to say the arrangement of the larger unities in plane and space, was subject to radical alterations: in Cézanne's pictures there is no longer any composition in the ordinary sense of the word, and this is one of the most revolutionary transformations in the history of the development of painting. One might almost believe that with his 'consolidation of impressionism', Cézanne created a new form of monumentality. The lack of composition in impressionistic works is only apparent; in reality the broad form of the composition is only concealed by the impressionistic method of painting, but in Cézanne its values have been definitely reduced.

That Cézanne often 'composed' very obviously, especially in many of his freely invented figure paintings and also in landscapes and still-lifes, is no real contradiction to the above statement. If we consider a number of Cézanne's pictorial compositions in themselves, without taking into account the role assigned to the compositional arrangement, in relation to the formation of the details, in the picture as a whole, we discover that there are a great number of variations: together with concealed compositions and those which seem to be without definite intention, we also find others with a simplicity and obviousness of compositional arrangement which is often almost schematic, with stress laid on symmetry or parallel lines. It is precisely in this variability and the sometimes excessive obviousness of the linear composition that we recognize its novelty and its, on the whole, secondary importance. In fact we can trace in Cézanne's work the changes in the significance of the composition: in the dark fantastic figure pictures, built up on sharp contrasts, of the early period, in which Cézanne sometimes appears to be making fun not only of his subject but also of the traditional forms of composition, these forms are nevertheless of decisive importance for the effect of the picture. But when, later, he continually used them in figure scenes, the emphasis was transferred to the structural forms he himself had created, which destroyed not only the forms and formulas of 'idealistic' figure-construction, but composition in general.

The principal specific characteristics here mentioned as forming part of Cézanne's pictorial method are very well suited to serve as elements for the construction of an abstract painting. And really one way taken by the followers of Cézanne led to the same end. But in the art of the master himself these characteristics have not this function; on the contrary all the effects of the relations of form, all the life of the pictorial organism, which is created out of the wealth of modulations of colour, out of the reciprocal reactions of plane and space, is brought into relation with the world of objects and serves to create objects. In Cézanne a pictorial world seems to have been created with the primary elements of vision; and it is in his painting that this occurred for the first time, not in impressionism, in which, however near it may come with its great creations to Cézanne's form of construction, many non-painteresque elements nevertheless contribute to the effect of the picture. Representations of the elementals, it is true, are continually found in the development of art – in the early years and at the height of the Middle Ages, in the art of Giotto, of Pieter Bruegel the Elder, of El Greco and of Rembrandt – but never have they been revealed so openly in the constituents of reality as in the painting of Cézanne, and never, except in his work, without being brought into relationship to some realm of thought, either generally religious or subjective, transcending reality.

Hardly any of the characteristics of Cézanne's art which have been mentioned in this brief summary are to be found in the works he produced at the beginning of his artistic career; in fact the pictures he painted up to the beginning of the seventies are characterized by features directly opposed to those we have enumerated.

A small number of oil paintings of various kinds, beneath the crudeness of which personal characteristics are barely discernible, have been preserved as the earliest works of the master. They were painted round about 1860. Cézanne – who was born on 19 January 1839 – was then about twenty and had not yet definitely adopted painting as his career. His father, Louis-Auguste Cézanne, a banker of Aix-en-Provence, was a strict man who did not approve at all of his son's intention to embrace the uncertain profession of a painter. However, he allowed him to study painting at the art school in Aix, but determined that as soon as his son had passed through the Collège Bourbon, he should take up the study of law. In 1861, nevertheless, Paul Cézanne succeeded in obtaining his father's permission to visit Paris, where he wanted to devote himself entirely to painting. Émile Zola, who had moved from Aix to Paris a few years before, was instrumental in persuading him to this decision. They had known each other as children and a romantic friendship sprang up in youth between the two, a friendship in which Baptistin Baille, who later became an engineer, participated. We find a clear and animated picture of this friendship in their letters and in the literary treatment which Zola gave to it in his books. The two artists remained close friends for several decades, until in 1886, after gradually drifting apart, they definitely broke off their relationship.

Cézanne's first stay in Paris, where he studied at the Académie Suisse, was not a long one. In the same year he returned discouraged to Aix and entered his father's banking business, though only for a short time. A few boyish drawings from the nude, now in the museum at Aix, have remained as examples of his artistic activity at that time. In 1862 he was in Paris again and in the following years he painted sometimes there, sometimes in his native town or at L'Estaque, near Marseilles. The pictures which Cézanne painted about the middle and in the second half of the sixties have a variety which shows clearly how he was striving to attain a personal style. Not only did he strive passionately, he actually succeeded in achieving a personal style, a style of emphatic, over-emphatic personality. Seldom has the hostility to the current artistic tendencies of a painter seeking his form, and a new form, found such vigorous expression as in these works of Cézanne's early period. Although it is often easy enough to see from which contemporaries these paintings drew their inspiration – from Courbet, Delacroix, Monticelli, and a little, in the later phase of this period of development, from Manet – most of them with their brutality and passion, in their choice of subject and form, give the impression of hostility to everything and everybody. Works of this kind are the large figure compositions, painted on the walls of the 'Jas de Bouffan', his parents' country house to the west of Aix, and also the series of portraits, in pure spatula technique – Cézanne's favourite technique at this period – of the so-called Uncle Dominique, the portrait of the painter Achille Emperaire, and a number of animated figure compositions often of weird and grotesque subjects. These pictures, created at a time of realism and incipient impressionism, at times appear like the works of a solitary expressionist, like caricatures of Baroque compositions. (Among the old masters, it is the great Venetians, whom Cézanne revered throughout his life, Ribera and Zurbarán, of whom we are reminded in the figure scenes which he painted at this time.) In the outlines and the modelling, and in the system of relationships of the colours with the extensive patches of chiaroscuro, these pictures often seem like rough versions of paintings by Daumier. The pictorial construction is generally of such a kind that large colour silhouettes are placed close together in sharp contrasts, before a spatial background usually of dark colour, as, for example, in the painting of *Christ's Descent into Limbo* from the 'Jas de Bouffan', in which the chalk-white flesh and the scarlet of Christ's mantle stand out against the blacks of the background.

But this is not his only form of painting in these years. Painted in 1866 or just after, his portrait of his father reading a newspaper – he is reading a copy of *L'Événement*, which published in that year Zola's celebrated polemic on art, *Mon Salon*, afterwards dedicated to Cézanne – which reveals strong reminiscences of the painting of Courbet, displays an entirely different treatment of colour. As regards colouring, several pictures painted from about 1870 to 1872 form a group of their own, characterized by a strongly marked scale of grey and brown tones, as, for example, the interior with a girl playing the piano, the figure composition, dated 1870, with the sailing-boat, the winter landscape at L'Estaque, where Cézanne lived during the Franco-Prussian war (Plate 6), and the view of the *Halle aux Vins* (Plate 7). One thing is common to all these pictures of his early period: a remarkable power in the application of colour. These works thus already contain a presage of what was later to become the most characteristic element in his art. The colour is still bound up with chiaroscuro and obstructed by the blackness of heavy, graphically outlined shadows, but is sometimes freed from them, as, for example, in some parts of the landscape with the railway cutting (Plate 8).

About this time Cézanne again changed his place of residence, and entered upon a new and important phase in his artistic development. In 1872, Hortense Fiquet, who became his wife, bore him a son in Paris. In the same year Cézanne went to Pontoise and Auvers-sur-Oise, where he remained working in the company of Camille Pissarro until 1874. There he also made the acquaintance of Dr Paul Gachet, later the friend of Van Gogh. The use of the term impressionism as applied to Cézanne's painting even at this period is certainly questionable. Many of his floral still-lifes and some of his landscapes, such as the view of the *Halle aux Vins*, dated 1872, can certainly be called impressionistic in many respects, but hardly a picture by Cézanne exists which one could unhesitatingly assign to a group of real impressionist pictures, for example a collection of landscapes by Pissarro, Monet and Sisley, as possessing fundamentally the same characteristics. In many of these pictures by Cézanne there is still too much of the form of the preceding period, especially in his *Maison du Pendu*, which was shown at the Impressionist exhibition held in 1874. The shut-in masses of the houses and of the terrain in the foreground still remind us of the 'walled' type of painting of the preceding years, and especially of the *Railway Cutting*, but the lightness of the colouring is not impressionistic, it already contains essential characteristics of Cézanne's specific colour treatment. This is true also of the later pictures from this period, in which the block-like solidity is abandoned and the looser construction and lighter colouring represent a distinct approach to impressionistic effects: in proportion as the contours, the modelling and chiaroscuro are replaced by the homogeneous impressionistic brushwork, the structure of the colouring, based on small component parts, acquires a new solidity. In the course of Cézanne's development, a constant return to his own older forms and a juxtaposition of different methods of painting are characteristic, and this peculiarity, which makes the arrangement of his works in chronological order so difficult, is particularly frequent in the works which he produced from about 1874 to near the end of the seventies. In the famous still-life with the fruit-dish in the Lecomte Collection, which can be dated at the end of the seventies, we have probably the first picture in which Cézanne achieves his ultimate pictorial form (Plate 12). Naturally his art undergoes plenty of changes even after this, but we can nevertheless speak of a certain definitiveness, for the most important principles of representation and form remain from this time on unaltered.

The pictures which Cézanne submitted to the Impressionist exhibitions of 1874 and 1877 were rejected in so vehement a manner that he took no further part in such exhibitions. As his continual efforts to be allowed to exhibit in the official Salon met with no success – with the exception of that held in 1882 – his activity remained unnoticed until the great comprehensive exhibition organized in 1895 by Ambroise Vollard.

Cézanne returned to work in Auvers several times after his long stay there, and he also worked in Pontoise, in Paris and the environs of the capital. In 1878 he was in L'Estaque again, and during the following years lived in various places in Provence and the North, in Paris, with Zola at Médan, at Melun and other places in the Ile-de-France. This continual change of scene went on until the last years of his life. In 1885 and 1886 he made long stays at Gardanne, to the south of Aix, where he painted a series of views of the town. A subject which he constantly returned to during his stays in Aix was the 'Jas de Bouffan', its buildings, its garden, its avenue of chestnuts and its pond (Plates 23, 28). The series of pictures of cardplayers and smokers, about 1890 (Plates 30, 31), was likewise painted at the 'Jas de Bouffan'. Soon after the death of his mother in 1897, the 'Jas de Bouffan' was sold and Cézanne moved into the town. From the middle of the nineties a certain landscape zone to the east of Aix had special significance for him: the curious building of the so-called 'Château Noir' and its surroundings (Plate 46), the woods with their peculiar rock-formations, the neighbouring 'Bibémus' quarry, and the views of Sainte-Victoire from this direction. In 1902 Cézanne built himself an atelier to the north of Aix, at 'Les Lauves'. In the landscapes painted during the master's last years, the Mont Sainte-Victoire is found again and again; as a mountain massif towering above the surrounding hilly country, it made a particularly effective subject for painting (Plates 24, 25, 47, 48a, 48b).

In addition to the pictures painted directly from nature, Cézanne constantly created invented figure compositions, mostly 'Bathers' (Plates 13, 40), but sometimes also allegorical scenes such as the *Apotheosis of Delacroix* and the two versions of the *Apotheosis of Woman*. Pictures of this kind give the most striking evidence of the continuance of tendencies found in his early paintings. The most important examples of his study of the problem of large figure compositions are the 'Baigneuses' painted in his last years, of which two smaller versions exist in addition to the one in the Philadelphia Museum (Plates 41–4).

Though still difficult, the chronological order of the pictures painted during his last phase can be established rather more clearly, for, in addition to the motive groups and landscapes mentioned above, several of his principal works can be dated, for example the portraits of Gustave Geffroy (1895), of Henri and Joachim Gasquet (1896/7), of Ambroise Vollard (1899; Plate 35), and the various portraits of the gardener Vallier, created in 1906, the last year of his life (Plate 45).

Except for a few interruptions – a visit to Western Switzerland in 1891 (the only time he went abroad), a journey to the lake of Annecy for the sake of his health in 1896 (Plate 37), stays in Paris and its environs (Montgeroult in 1899, Fontainebleau in 1904 and 1905) – Cézanne spent the closing years of his life in Aix.

His proud and assertive solitude, with its foundations in the peculiarities of his temperament – shyness and explosions of violence, weakness and inaptitude in dealing with everyday matters, distrustfulness and irritability – now degenerated into the loneliness of old age. A whole series of anecdotes – many of them of dubious authenticity – has sprung up concerning the external appearance at that time of this ever restless and incalculable man, always tortured by doubts of his own ability; often the desire to give literary interest to the many obscure peculiarities of his temperament and his artistic life had hindered rather than helped the discernment of the truth, and stereotyped judgements such as that of the 'queer' Cézanne have led to mischievous exaggerations and distortions of the truth.

In his last years signs of outward success and recognition at last came to Cézanne. At first he accepted them suspiciously, but later they gave him cause to hope that a younger generation might carry on his work. He thought it necessary to go on working intensively until the last day of his life, in order that he might carry his work, which still seemed to him to present so many unsolved problems, still farther. Repeatedly, in the letters written in his last years, he speaks of 'some progress' which, he has succeeded in making. His last pictures – landscapes of the Sainte-Victoire, the 'Château Noir' and the Arc valley – which represent the zenith of his own achievements and are masterpieces of pictorial creation in general, were painted while he was struggling against illness and exhaustion, as can be seen from the letters which he wrote to his son Paul during the last weeks. His son, who was bound to him by the ties of a deep affection, and several friends both young and old were with him during the last years: a friend of his youth, the sculptor Philippe Solari – the prototype of Mahoudeau in Zola's *L'Oeuvre* – with his son Émile; Henri Gasquet, another contemporary, and his son Joachim; the painters Émile Bernard and Charles Camoin; and the writer, Léo Larguier. It is from the reminiscences of Joachim Gasquet, Bernard, Camoin and Larguier that the picture of the master's outward appearance and life has been handed down to us.

On 15 October 1906, Cézanne was overtaken by a heavy storm of rain while working on a picture; he was brought back unconscious to his house in the Rue Boulegon, and died there a few days later, on 22 October.

Outline Biography

1839 19 January: Paul Cézanne born at Aix-en-Provence, the son of a well-to-do banker, Louis-Auguste Cézanne.

1852–8 A student at the Collège Bourbon at Aix. Begins a close friendship with fellow student, Émile Zola, that lasts until 1886. With Baille and Numa Coste they form a tightly knit group.

1858 Zola leaves Aix for Paris, returning in the holidays with encouraging reports of life in the capital. Cézanne is tempted to go there, but remains in Aix. Gains the *baccalauréat* at the second attempt. Works in the Academy of Drawing at Aix.

1859–61 At Law School, Aix, in compliance with his father's wishes.

1859 'Jas de Bouffan' purchased by Louis-Auguste Cézanne.

1861 Abandons law to follow an artistic career. In April pays his first visit to Paris, living first in the Rue Coquillière, later in the Rue des Feuillantines. September (?): returns, discouraged, to Aix; begins work in the family bank of Cézanne and Cabassol.

1862 November (?): rejoins Zola in Paris, where he remains, making occasional visits home, until 1870. Apparently fails entrance examinations for the École des Beaux-Arts.

1863 Exhibits at the notorious *Salon des Refusés*. Works at the Atelier Suisse, where he meets Guillaumin, Francisco Oller y Cestero and Guillemet.

1864 Rejected at the Salon: this will become a regular occurrence.

1865 Zola publishes *La Confession de Claude*, dedicated to Cézanne and Baille.

1866 Complimented by Manet on one of his still-lifes. Rejected at the Salon in spite of the intervention of Daubigny. Writes letter to the Director of Fine Arts, the reactionary Comte de Nieuwerkerke. Praised by Zola in *L'Événement*, for which Zola had become art critic.

1867 Exhibits a painting in Marseilles, but it has to be withdrawn to prevent it being attacked by the crowd.

1870 Avoids being drafted on the outbreak of the Franco-Prussian War. Works at L'Estaque and lives with Hortense Fiquet, whom he had met the previous year.

1871 Returns to Paris after the end of the Commune.

1872 Hortense gives birth to a son, who is christened Paul. Goes to Pontoise, where he works alongside Pissarro, one of whose landscapes he carefully copies.

1873 At Auvers-sur-Oise he meets Dr Gachet, one of the first patrons of the Impressionists. Paints *A Modern Olympia* (Plate 3).

1874 At Pissarro's insistence, he is admitted to the Impressionist Group Exhibition, to which he contributes three pictures, including *A Modern Olympia*.

1875 Meets Victor Chocquet, whose portrait he paints, and who buys one of his pictures.

1876 In Aix and L'Estaque for the greater part of the year.

1877 Shows sixteen works (mostly landscapes and still-lifes) at the third Impressionist Exhibition; they are badly received.

1878 In Aix, L'Estaque and Marseilles. Accepts help from Zola because of financial difficulties with his father, who finds out about the secret liaison with Hortense.

1879–81 Works at Médan, where Zola has a house; also at Melun, in Paris and again with Pissarro (and Gauguin) at Pontoise.

1882 Admitted to the Salon as a 'pupil of Guillemet'.

1883–5 At Aix and L'Estaque, with visits to Paris.

1886 March: publication of Zola's *L'Oeuvre*, a novel that contains references which deeply hurt Cézanne and which lead to the complete breakdown of their friendship. 28 April: Cézanne and Hortense Fiquet are married at Aix. 23 October: death of Louis-Auguste Cézanne, who leaves his son well provided for.

1889 Victor Chocquet uses his influence to have Cézanne's *Maison du Pendu* shown at the Exposition Universelle.

1890 Three pictures by Cézanne exhibited – by invitation – by *Les XX* in Brussels. Begins to suffer from diabetes.

1891–4 In Aix and in Paris.

1891 About this time he becomes a devout Catholic.

1895 December: large exhibition of Cézanne's paintings organized by the dealer, Vollard; it is from this moment that the painter's fame dates.

1896 April: meeting with Joachim Gasquet, the first of a group of young admirers who gather round the painter in the last years of his life.

1897–9 Working in Aix, Paris, Fontainebleau and Pontoise. Two of Cézanne's paintings are hung in the Berlin National Gallery but are banned by the Kaiser. In the Dreyfus Affair, Cézanne disapproves of the stand taken by Zola.

1899 Three pictures by Cézanne exhibited at Salon des Indépendants.

1900 Three pictures exhibited at the Paris Centennial Exposition.

1900–6 Aix the centre of his activities.

1902 November: purchases property on 'Chemin des Lauves' for a studio. Maurice Denis's *Hommage à Cézanne* shown at the Salon.

1906 Ten pictures exhibited at Salon d'Automne. 22 October: dies in Aix.

List of Plates

1. *Portrait of Achille Emperaire.* 200 × 122 cm. About 1866–8. Signed. Private Collection.
2. *The Orgy.* 130 × 81 cm. About 1866–8. Private Collection.
3. *A Modern Olympia.* 46 × 56 cm. About 1873. Paris, Louvre.
   The theme of a 'Modern Olympia', an ironical allusion to Manet's famous *Olympia* of 1863, was treated by Cézanne in two oil paintings and one watercolour. The version here reproduced was at one time in the possession of Dr Paul Gachet at Auvers-sur-Oise.
4. *The Temptation of St Anthony.* 57 × 76 cm. About 1869–70. Zürich, E. G. Bührle Foundation.
   The earliest surviving version of this subject in Cézanne's œuvre; two later versions have also been preserved.
5. *The Black Marble Clock.* 55 × 74 cm. About 1869–70. Paris, Stavros S. Niarchos Collection.
   This painting was formerly owned by Émile Zola.
6. *Melting Snow at l'Estaque.* 73 × 92 cm. About 1870–1. Zürich, E. G. Bührle Foundation.
7. *The 'Halle aux Vins' in Paris.* 73 × 92 cm. 1872. Private Collection.
   The painting shows the view from the flat in the Rue Jussieu, where Cézanne lived from December 1871 until the summer of 1872.
8. *The Railway Cutting.* 80 × 129 cm. About 1871. Munich, State Gallery.
   In the foreground the garden wall of the 'Jas de Bouffan', in the background the Montagne Sainte-Victoire.
9. *The Bridge of Maincy.* 58 × 73 cm. 1879. Paris, Louvre.
10. Detail from *The Railway Cutting* (Plate 8).
11. Detail from *The Bridge of Maincy* (Plate 9).
12. *Still-Life.* 46 × 55 cm. About 1877–9. Private Collection.
13. *Three Bathing Women.* 50 × 50 cm. About 1879–82. Paris, Petit Palais.
    One of the early versions of the subject of 'Bathers', which recurs throughout Cézanne's career and culminates in the monumental versions of his last years, cf. Plates 40–44.
14. *Self-Portrait.* 33 × 24 cm. About 1880. Winterthur, Oskar Reinhart Collection.
15. *Self-Portrait.* Detail in original size (55 × 47 cm.). About 1880. Munich, State Gallery.
16. *Cézanne's Son, Paul.* 65 × 54 cm. 1885. Washington, D.C., National Gallery of Art, Chester Dale Collection.
17. *Portrait of Madame Cézanne.* 93 × 73 cm. About 1881–2. Zürich, E. G. Bührle Foundation.
    Cézanne painted many portraits of his wife. Cf. Plate 33.
18. *Self-Portrait with Palette.* 92 × 73 cm. About 1885–7. Zürich, E. G. Bührle Foundation.
19. *View of Gardanne ('Les trois moulins').* 92 × 73 cm. About 1885–6. Brooklyn, N.Y., Museum.
    This picture is obviously unfinished, but in the case of many other oil paintings by Cézanne it is doubtful, and has been disputed, whether or not they have been completed. The title '*Les trois moulins*' refers to the cylindrical foundations of three windmills on the hill at the left.
20. *Still-Life.* 43 × 54 cm. About 1879. Copenhagen, Royal Museum.
21. *Still-Life.* 71 × 91 cm. About 1883–7. Munich, State Gallery.
22. *The Bay of Marseilles seen from l'Estaque.* 76 × 97 cm. About 1885. Chicago, Art Institute.
    The landscape round the Bay of Marseilles, particularly the surroundings of l'Estaque, forms the subject of many of Cézanne's oil paintings and watercolours, extending from about 1870 to 1890. Cf. Plate 6.
23. *The 'Jas de Bouffan'.* 60 × 73 cm. About 1885–7. Prague, National Gallery.
    The 'Jas de Bouffan', built in the late seventeenth century and added to in the eighteenth, was the country estate of Cézanne's parents on the south-western outskirts of Aix. The artist painted and drew many views of the house and of motifs in the garden – particularly an avenue of chestnut trees and a pond – and in the immediate surroundings (e.g. the *Railway Cutting*, Plate 8).
24. *Montagne Sainte-Victoire.* 60 × 73 cm. About 1885–7. Washington, D.C., Phillips Collection.

The extensive mountain range of the Sainte-Victoire is one of the most important motifs in Cézanne's landscape paintings. The mountain can be found in some of his early works (cf. Plate 8), but became a favourite subject in his last decade, when he was painting near the 'Château Noir' (Plate 46) and near his studio in the 'Lauves', which was built in 1902 (Plates 47, 48a, 48b). In the present picture and in Plate 25, as well as in some other paintings, the mountain range is seen from 'Bellevue', south of Aix, where his brother-in-law, Maxime Conil, owned a farm.

25. *Landscape with Viaduct: Montagne Sainte-Victoire*. 65 × 82 cm. About 1885–7. New York, Metropolitan Museum of Art (H. O. Havemeyer Collection).

26. *The Blue Vase*. 61 × 50 cm. About 1885–7. Paris, Louvre.

27. *Still-Life* (detail). 64 × 81 cm. About 1888–90. Paris, Louvre.

28. *Chestnut Trees at the 'Jas de Bouffan'*. 73 × 92 cm. About 1885–7. Minneapolis, Institute of Arts, William H. Dunwoody Fund. See note on Plate 23.

29. *Aqueduct and Lock*. 74 × 93 cm. About 1888–90. Paris, Stavros S. Niarchos Collection.

30. *The Card Players*. 60 × 73 cm. About 1892. London, Courtauld Institute Galleries.
The subject of the 'Card Players' was treated in a group of five oil paintings and a few studies. These pictures were painted at the 'Jas de Bouffan' about 1892.

31. *Man Smoking a Pipe*. 73 × 60 cm. About 1892. London, Courtauld Institute Galleries.

32. *The Boy in the Red Waistcoat*. 79 × 64 cm. About 1890–4. Zürich, E. G. Bührle Foundation.
The same model, a young Italian, was portrayed by Cézanne in three further oil paintings and one watercolour.

33. *Madame Cézanne in a Yellow Armchair*. 81 × 65 cm. About 1890–4. Chicago, Art Institute.

34. *The Woman with the Coffee-Pot*. 130 × 96 cm. About 1890–4. Paris, Louvre.

35. *Portrait of Ambroise Vollard*. 100 × 81 cm. 1899. Paris, Petit Palais.
The sitter, a well-known art dealer, has devoted a chapter of his book on Cézanne to the genesis of this portrait. This is often quoted as an instance of how slowly the artist worked, for according to Vollard, Cézanne abandoned the portrait after one hundred and fifteen sittings, with the remark that he was 'not altogether displeased with the shirt'.

36. *Colline des Pauvres*. 81 × 65 cm. About 1895. New York, Metropolitan Museum of Art.
A building, now rebuilt, on the estate 'Saint-Joseph', originally owned by the Jesuits, near the road to Le Tholonet. On the slope behind lies the quarry 'Bibémus', where Cézanne painted several landscapes during the years around 1900.

37. *The Lake of Annecy*. 65 × 81 cm. London, Courtauld Institute Galleries.
In the summer of 1896, Cézanne stayed at Talloires near Annecy.

38. *Still-Life*. 53 × 71 cm. About 1892–4. London, Tate Gallery.

39. *Dish of Peaches*. 31 × 40 cm. About 1896. Winterthur, Oskar Reinhart Collection.

40. *Bathers*. 22 × 32 cm. About 1890–4. Paris, Louvre.

41. *Bathing Women*. 51 × 62 cm. About 1900–5. Chicago, Art Institute.

42. *Bathing Women*. 130 × 193 cm. About 1900–5. London, National Gallery.

43–44. *Bathing Women*. 208 × 249 cm. About 1900–5. Philadelphia, Museum of Art, Wilstach Collection.
In this painting, the largest version of his compositions of nude figures. Cézanne has achieved the monumentality of a mural painting. Work on his last paintings of bathing women occupied him for many years, and at his death he left them unfinished.

45. *The Gardener*. 65 × 55 cm. About 1906. London, Tate Gallery.
In his last years Cézanne painted several portraits of his gardener Vallier.

46. *The 'Château Noir'*. 73 × 92 cm. About 1904. Winterthur, Oskar Reinhart Collection.
The 'Château Noir' was built around the middle of the last century, but remained unfinished. Around 1900 Cézanne painted many pictures of the building and of motifs in the surrounding forest.

47. *Montagne Sainte-Victoire*. 65 × 81 cm. About 1904–6. Zürich, E. G. Bührle Foundation.

48a. *Montagne Sainte-Victoire*. Watercolour, 36 × 55 cm. About 1904–6. London, Tate Gallery.

48b. *Montagne Sainte-Victoire*. Oil, unfinished. 73 × 54 cm. About 1904–6. Basle, Galerie Beyeler.

The publishers wish to express their gratitude to the private owners and public galleries for permission to reproduce the paintings listed above.
The illustrations were selected by Ludwig Goldscheider, London.

1. *Portrait of Achille Emperaire*. About 1866–8. Private Collection

2. *The Orgy*. About 1866–8. Private Collection

A Modern Olympia. About 1873. Paris, Louvre

6 *Melting Snow at l'Estaque.* About 1870–1, Zürich, E. G. Bührle Foundation

8. *The Railway Cutting. About* 1871. Munich, State Gallery

10. Detail from *The Railway Cutting* (Plate 8)

11. Detail from *The Bridge of Maincy* (Plate 9)

12. *Still-Life.*
About 1877–9.
Private Collection

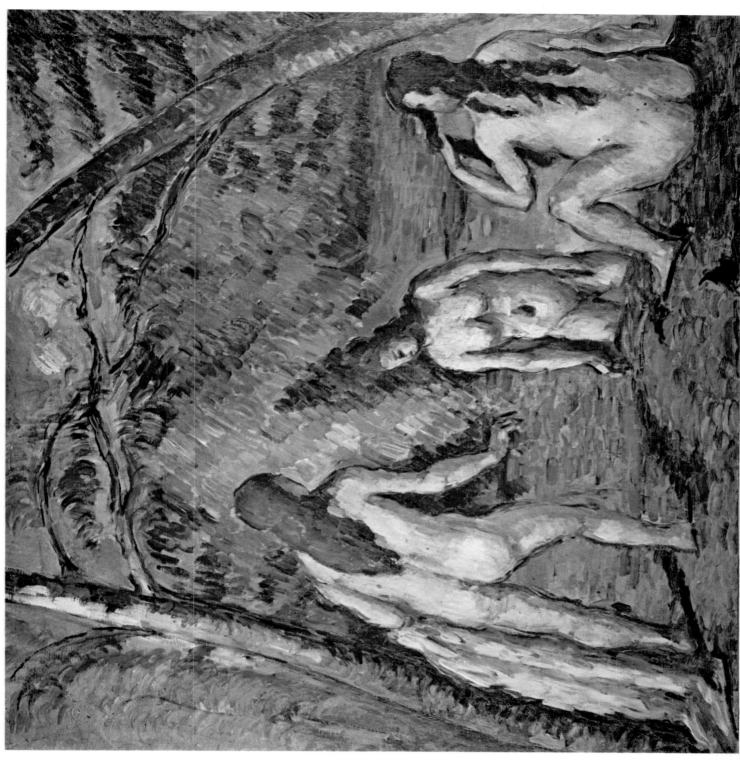

13. *Three Bathing Women.* About
1879–82. Paris, Petit Palais

14. *Self-Portrait*. About 1880. Winterthur, Oskar Reinhart Collection

15. *Self-Portrait*. About 1880. Detail in original size. Munich, State Gallery

16. *Cézanne's Son, Paul*. 1885. Washington, D.C., National Gallery of Art, Chester Dale Collection

17. *Portrait of Madame Cézanne*. About 1881–2. Zürich, E. G. Bührle Foundation

18. *Self-Portrait with Palette*. About 1885–7. Zürich, E. G. Bührle Foundation

9. *View of Gardanne ('Les trois moulins')*. About 1885–6. Brooklyn, N.Y., Museum

20. *Still-Life*. About 1879. Copenhagen, Royal Museum

1. *Still-Life*. About 1883–7. Munich, State Gallery

38   *The Bay of Marseilles seen from l'Estaque.* About 1885. Chicago, Art Institute

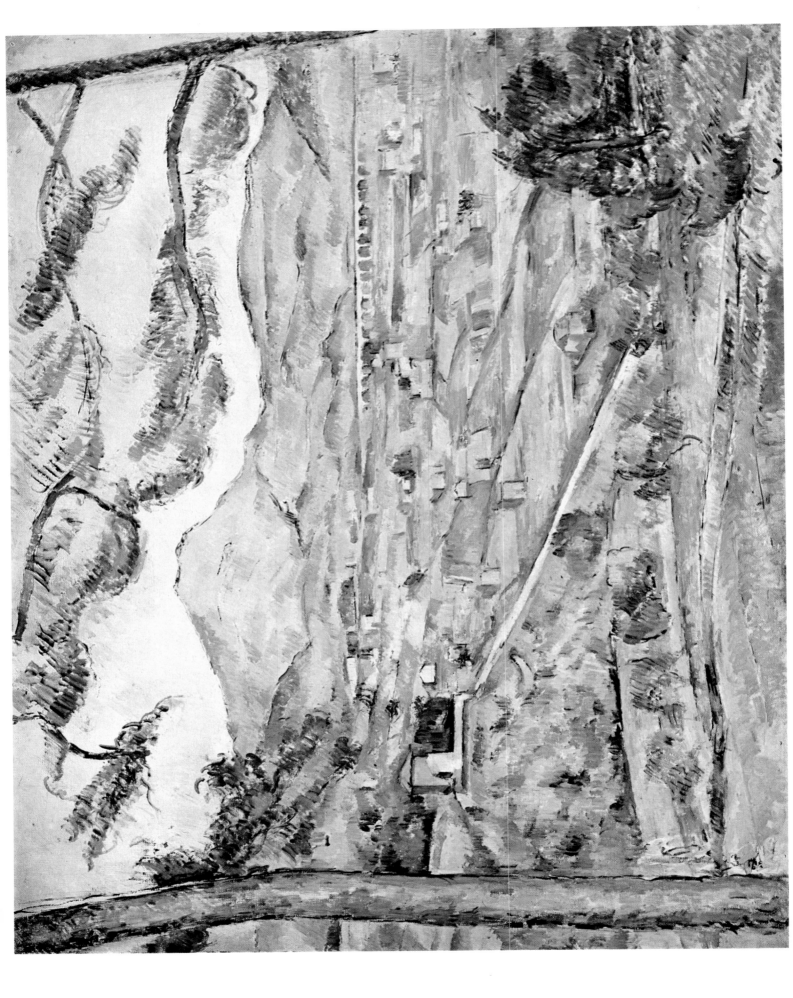

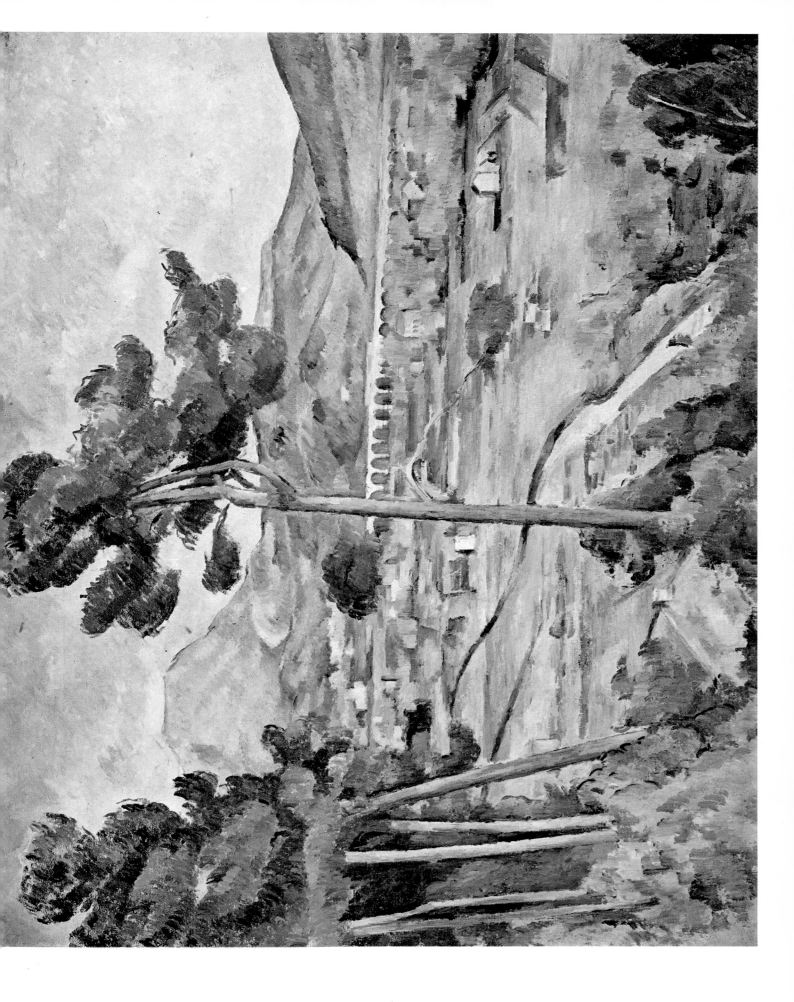

26. *The Blue Vase*. About 1885–7. Paris, Louvre

27. *Still-Life* (detail). About 1888–90. Paris, Louvre

28 *Chestnut Trees at the 'Jas de Bouffan'* About 1885–7 Minneapolis Institute of Arts. William H. Dunwoody Fund

29. *Aqueduct and Lock*. About 1888–90. Paris, Stavros S. Niarchos Collection

30. *The Card Players*. About 1892. London, Courtauld Institute Galleries

31. *Man Smoking a Pipe*. About 1892. London, Courtauld Institute Galleries

32. *The Boy in the Red Waistcoat*. About 1890–4. Zürich, E.G. Bührle Foundation

Madame Cézanne in a Yellow Armchair. About 1890–4. Chicago, Art Institute

34. *The Woman with the Coffee-Pot*. About 1890–4. Paris, Louvre

35. *Portrait of Ambroise Vollard.* 1899. Paris, Petit Palais

40. *Bathers*. About 1890–4. Paris, Louvre

42. *Bathing Women*. About 1900–5. London, National Gallery

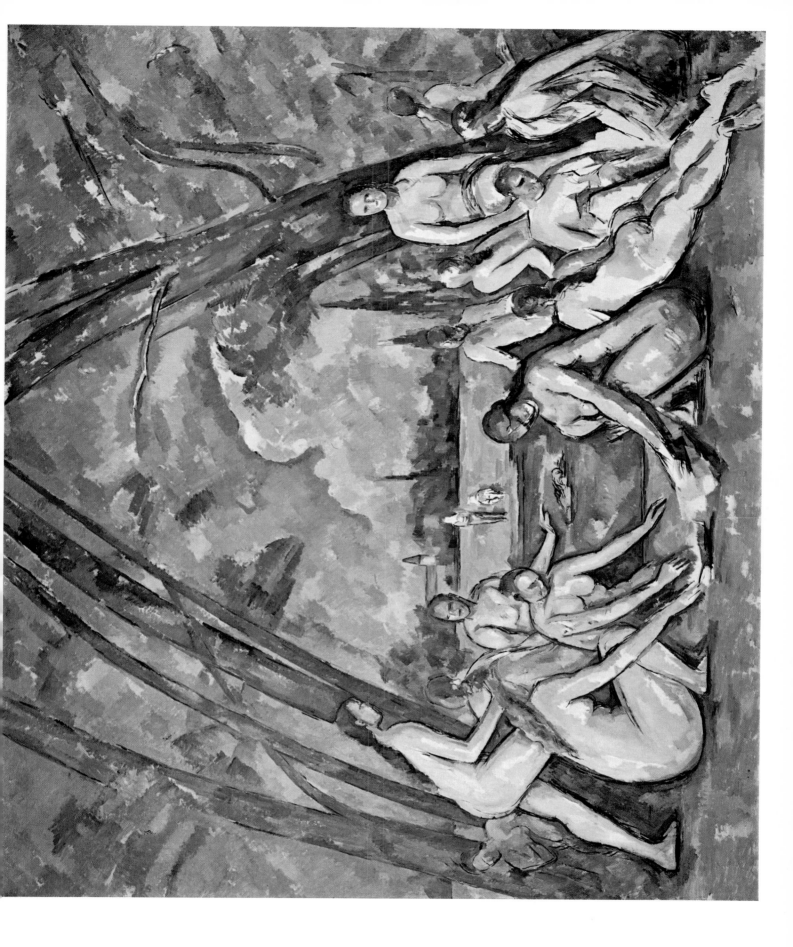

44. Detail from *Bathing Women* (Plate 43)

45. *The Gardener*. About 1906. London, Tate Gallery

46. The 'Château Noir'. About 1904. Winterthur, Oskar Reinhart Collection

48a. *Montagne Sainte-Victoire*. Watercolour. About 1904–6. London, Tate Gallery

48b. *Montagne Sainte-Victoire*. Oil, unfinished. About 1904–6. Basle, Galerie Beyeler